OUTLIVING

Bernard O'Donoghue

Chatto & Windus
LONDON

Published by Chatto & Windus 2003

2 4 6 8 10 9 7 5 3

First published in Great Britain in 2003 by
Chatto & Windus
Random House, 20 Vauxhall Bridge Road,
London SW1V 2SA

Random House Australia (Pty) Limited
20 Alfred Street, Milsons Point, Sydney,
New South Wales 2061, Australia

Random House New Zealand Limited
18 Poland Road, Glenfield,
Auckland 10, New Zealand

Random House South Africa (Pty) Limited
Endulini, 5A Jubilee Road, Parktown 2193, South Africa

The Random House Group Limited Reg. No. 954009
www.randomhouse.co.uk

A CIP catalogue record for this book
is available from the British Library

ISBN 0 7011 7481 1

Papers used by Random House are natural,
recyclable products made from wood grown in sustainable forests.
The manufacturing processes conform to the environmental
regulations of the country of origin.

Typeset by Deltatype Ltd, Birkenhead, Merseyside
Printed and bound in Great Britain by
Mackays of Chatham, PLC

For my neighbours in Cullen and Millstreet

ACKNOWLEDGEMENTS

I am grateful to the editors of the following publications where some of these poems first appeared: *Atlanta Review*, *Canadian Journal of Irish Studies*, *A Chatter of Choughs* (ed. Lucy Newlyn), *The Canary River Review*, *The Cork Examiner*, *The Cork Literary Review*, *The Guardian*, *The Irish Times*, *The New Statesman*, *The Observer*, *Poetry Ireland Review*, *PN Review*, *Poetry Scotland*, *The Reader*, *Thumbscrew*, *The Times Literary Supplement*, *West 47*, *Oxford Poetry*, *The Oxford Magazine*, *The Shop*, *Stephen's Green*.

'The Day I Outlived My Father' was Clutag Poetry Leaflet No. 3, printed by Andrew McNeillie; 'The Quiet Man' was prefixed to Luke Gibbons *The Quiet Man* (Cork University Press); 'Philomela' was published in *Last Words*, edited by Don Paterson and Jo Shapcott; 'Goalkeepers' was published in *The Living Stream: a Festschrift for Theo Dorgan*, edited by Niamh Morris; 'The Potato-Gatherers' was written in response to George Russell (AE)'s painting of that name, and published in *A Conversation Piece: Poetry and Art*, edited by Adrian Rice and Angela Reid; 'In Millstreet Hospital' was written for *The Gift*, an anthology of writings for the National Health Service, compiled by David Morley; 'Growing Up With Cullen Feis' was published in the centenary programme for Cullen Feis, edited by Brenda O'Sullivan and Susan O'Connor; 'Islandmagee Castle' was written for *Poetry in Motion* (New Belfast Community Arts Initiative, co-ordinated by Joseph Sheehy); 'Fra Alberigo's Bad Fruit' was read at the Dante Project for Poetry International 2000 in the Purcell Room, organised by Maura Dooley.

CONTENTS

THE DAY I OUTLIVED MY FATHER

Yet no one sent me flowers, or even
asked me out for a drink. If anything
it makes it worse, your early death, that
having now at last outlived you, I too
have broken ranks, lacking maybe
the imagination to follow you
in investigating that other, older world.

So I am in new territory from here on:
must blaze my own trail, read alone
the hooftracks in the summer-powdered dust
and set a good face to the future:
at liberty at last like mad Arnaut
to cultivate the wind, to hunt the bull
on hare-back, to swim against the tide.

THE CITY AT SHRONE

A strange place for a city, Shrone, where
The mountain rain drifts along the western Pap
And the fields drain downwards to Rathmore.

Still, it is a strange city. One small house,
Single-chimneyed, whitewashed and tethered to
A disconnected ESB pole near the ramparts.

Half as old as time. The blessed virgin shelters
In her glass grotto, her blue mantle fading
Like the sky, the beads round her neck rusting.

Maybe, after all, it's not such a foolish place
For a city: its long-past citizens sleep well,
Unvisited by showers of high explosive.

April/May 1999

('The City' – *An Cathair* in Irish – is the name given to a small ring-fort near the mountains called The Paps in the Kerry-Cork borderlands.)

IN MILLSTREET HOSPITAL

My cousin, they tell me, doesn't wake up much,
nor does she seem to see the green mountain
framed in the window of this chapel of ease
for travellers booked in for their long pilgrimage.
When I leave at the end of visiting-hours
a small, tidy man is sitting by the door:
stick, well-knotted tie, watch-chain, tweed jacket.
He gets to his feet, raises his hat and enquires:
'Excuse my troubling you, but would you be
going anywhere near a railway station?'
The young smiling nurse bends over him,
and takes him by the elbow, saying:
'Maybe tomorrow, James. Maybe tomorrow
we'll take you to the station.'

ALZHEIMER FRUIT

In that underworld you ambled off to
On your own, you must have drunk or eaten
Something prohibited so that your memory
Of this life faded. But where could that place
Have been? And what was the fruit? If we knew,

We'd go there with you, or for you, and put it back:
Whatever it was you ate or drank or brought away.
I dreamt I came upon you in the early hours
In your pyjamas, scoring a sheet of paper
Over and over with a highlighter pen.

'This pen's gone dry,' you said. 'I'm trying my best
To make it orange up this paragraph.'

A CANDLE FOR DOLLY DUGGAN

Venice, Easter 2001

Improbabilities of course, we all
know that: that this graceful taper
I force into the tallowed cast iron
beneath the *Assumption* in the Frari
could change the heavens, so that she
can pick up her cigarettes and lighter
to move on to a higher circle, as before
she moved, talking, through the lanes of Cork.

Sir Thomas Browne said there aren't impossibilities
enough in religion for an active faith.
So I'll go on spending liras and francs
and pesetas across the smoky hush
of Catholic Europe until she says
'That's enough', and then I'm free to toast
her in red wine outside in the sunlit squares.

'THE HORSE THAT HAD VISIONS OF IMMORTALITY'

for George Jack

The painting, you reminded us, was abstract,
So we have to close our eyes in front of it
Before we can see a pattern and a line
In the movement of its colours. A painter
In West Cork sets up her easel by the shore,
Then copies what she sees inland, knowing
That behind her there stretches out
An inexhaustible expanse of ocean.

Open your eyes briefly, and try again
With this children's game. You mark an 'x'
On a sheet of paper, and a dot
Four inches away from it. As you move
The paper in and out before your eyes,
Always intent upon the dot, the 'x'
First goes and then appears again.
Or a last Piers Plowman's look, *perceiving*

More deeper, at a clutch of daffodils
Which toil upwards from the thick twists
Of greenwhite at their base to the lipsticks
Of their careful, skin-packaged heads.
A few days on, most of the flowers are still
In bloom, but one or two are drying. Why?
Faced with that question, all that we can do
Is close our eyes and wait for another vision.

TELEGRAMS

for Mick Henry

1. TWIST AND BUST

End of a day in the wet trench,
you're all so tired you can hardly pull
the boots off, but you have to
before the pub will let you in.
Polite notice: site footwear
not admitted.

On the dark table,
inside the digs front door:
the buff envelope, face down.
Whose father, sister, brother, mother
this time? Come on; leave it. Eat first,
play a hand of cards in the *Bell*,
face it after closing-time.

2. DELIVERY BOYS

Fogarty's kept his usual station at the bar
all night, with a good view of the swing doors
in the mirror in front of him. Two more
and he'll be off himself to catch
the second-last bus to Camden Town.

And then he sees them coming: two
workmates from the old days in Bristol,
but wearing ties. 'I know what's bringing
ye fuckers, and I don't want to hear about it.'

3. SAILING TICKETS

In high summer when they all went home,
numbers on the mailboat were controlled
by the issue of ten-shilling sailing tickets.
No getting on without them: that is except
if you could show an Irish telegram
to the man at the barrier: 'I must get back
for the funeral, sir; my mother's passed away.'
Sometimes of course she had; more times she hadn't.

THE QUIET MAN

One of the great films, by general consent,
It could have been called 'The Quiet American',
Or, for that matter, 'The Violent Irishman':
Trim John Wayne, not easily roused, but once roused
His vengeance a wonder of the western world,
With Maureen O'Hara, for all her wish
For independence, kicking impotently
On his shoulder. We saw it in Manchester,
On holiday from the hayfields of North Cork,
During the Korean War, at a time when films
Ran continuously. We came in, aptly enough,
At the culminating meadow fight,
Stayed for Tom and Jerry and the Pathé News,
Before leaving at the point we'd started at,
With McLaglan lying battered in the hay.

CLAIRE, PLAYING SCHUBERT

ye lovely ladyes with youre longe fingres

This is the kind of poem I never write,
dropping musicians' names. But where else
is there to turn, but back down the path
that leads to childhood and those dreamt despairs.
After the power of the closing bars
that made you thrust down at the keys, then lean
back to make the passion keep its distance,
your hands stay fixed, reluctant at the end
to leave their scene of triumph.

Dream-children,

of course. I've never heard you play. I know you less
than I know Uchida whom I saw once
taking the stairs two steps at a time,
hurrying to play Schubert in the Festival Hall,
on the floor above where I was reading.

TWO FIDDLERS AT SCULLY'S

For the higher notes, the fiddle lifts Tim Browne
By the chin clean off his seat, like a child
Hoisted by the jowls to see France or China.
But not painfully: you can tell that
By the small smile that never leaves his mouth
And the readiness to laugh behind his glasses.
Raymond hardly stirs: his eyes never shift
From his fiddle which he scrutinizes
In solemn puzzlement, nudging the music out
While Browne pulls it gallantly across himself.

NO MORE BOTHER TO HIM

i.m. Paul O'Flinn 14.3.2001

The red kites are very red this morning,
caught by the spring sun as they swing high
over Nuneham Courtenay, and in town
a wintered-over flycatcher skates out,
trying to keep his footing on the air.
So things are looking up at last it seems:
the floods receded, and the long winter's cold.

But on the eastern skyline, out past Bicester
a black pall hangs above the trees
where the cattle are burning, pyres no doubt
that we will see tonight replicated
over Tetovo on the News. There is
cause then for these red eyes all round,
light as Paul would have made of mourning him.

THE EDUCATING OF JIM FALLON

In the National School when we were doing reading,
I must have been looking out the window,
down over the glen below the road
at the big tree-lined circle of Ring's fort,
or listening for the thresher toiling past,
or half-asleep from being kept awake

by the corncrake's endless, useless nightly courting.
I still remember some things being read out:
'In Ireland long ago'; 'The stag at eve
had drunk his fill'; 'The boy who cried wolf';
the *Hispaniola* sailing gallantly from Bristol;
but I had no call for any of the lettering.

Forty years later though a workmate
in lunchbreaks at a building-site in Bristol
wrote for me on opened-out fag-boxes
in plain letters: *This be the verse you grave*
for me: 'Here he lies where he wants to be.
Home is the sailor, home from the sea.'

I hung them all around the digs walls,
where I could see them, shaving or smoking in bed.
We shook hands at Temple Meads when he set off
for the last time. Then, as the train pulled in,
the words all came back to me again:
'*And the hunter home from the hill,*'

I said to him there in everybody's hearing,
And asked 'Doesn't that poem beat everything?'

CONCORDIAM IN POPULO

And Duncan's horses . . . 'Tis said they ate each other

After the heart attack, prodigious events
Took place: neighbours who hadn't talked
For twenty years, because of trees cut down,
Horses gone lame, or cattle straying,
Cooperated in organizing lifts
To make arrangements for the funeral.

Husbands who'd not addressed a civil word
To wives for even longer referred to them
By christian name in everybody's hearing:
Lizzie or *Julanne* or *Nora May*.
The morning of the burial it rained and rained,
And we all huddled close by the graveside,

Trusting one another, small differences
Set aside, just as Kate had told us once
How she crept into bed when the thunder seemed
To throw giant wooden boxes at the house,
Beside the husband that she hadn't spoken to
Since the first month after their sorry wedding.

KERRY *V.* CAVAN, 1955

We're in a long single-storeyed farmhouse
at Ardmore, at the end of their era,
politely Sunday-visiting my mother's people
and listening to the Kerry–Cavan semi-final
in the anti-cyclone summer of '55.
The Kerry backs are fouling, fouling,
and my father, in opposition to
the kind women-teachers in that house,
cheered at the Cavan equalizing goal.
They, sitting in a well-dressed row, had clapped
at Kerry's goal, and I, swallowing tears,
told him off. 'Wait till I see Jerome O'Shea.'

There was someone else there too: the old man
we'd gone to visit, my mother's Uncle Danny.
He sat at the back, wearing a hat, mumbling
occasionally and pointing down urgently
at the concrete floor. The women-teachers – grown-ups –
sat or knelt beside him, rubbing his hands
and pleading, 'What is it, Dada?' I hardly knew
what to do with my eyes.

THE GRANARIES OF FINISTERRE

for Antonio Raul de Toro Santos

'Som men grave in tree, some in ston wal' (*Chaucer*)

In every village, right down to the Cape,
they're up on stilts, though varying in gravity.
Some, like teenagers that have outgrown
their strength, are gawky formulas composed
of wash-green slats; others are oat-cathedrals
in stone. Dialects, words or music, or
designs to win in love: it's all the same;
for every man that has a house to build
will not start off without reflection,
but first takes in the sky's elevation,
and what they've always done in that vicinity,
domestic architects for ten miles round
across the centuries, year in, year out.

The sea is never far away round here,
whether sheltering behind the boats at Malpica
or washing the grim rocks around the Sisargas.
Beyond those island-colonies of sea-birds,
each screeching its own special call,
what you'd eventually come to is an echo
of these pale grains in the matt pink grumble
of Lynch's thresher. Close your eyes; behind
the gulls it's 'Harvest Home', played Cullen-style,
here, where the square lighthouse of Coruña
recalls the fleets that once set out to brave
the storms in Bantry Bay and off Kinsale,
blown far away from the calendars of hope.

ARTISTIC BLOCK

The great Russian bass Shalyapin
woke up every morning, cleared his throat
and knew his voice was gone: this time for ever.
All through the day his wife cajoled
and comforted, feeding him balsams
and reminding him of past successes
until by 7 p.m. he's ready
once again to take the plaudits
while she fights off sleep in the dress circle.

DARKENING THE DOOR

I dreamt the house was broken
Into. But the items we noticed
Missing were things not there
In the first place:
Grandfather clock; gold rings; ornate boxes.

And then I thought I heard
What must be a great bird
Beating its wings behind the hedge:
But in the morning
Found it was flapping baling-plastic.

Every morning when I leave
I pause a second longer, reflecting
That this departure may be the last;
At each return
My arching shadow darkens the door.

Love, if something does go missing
From the house contents,
Rest assured that I know well enough
The thief
Is likelier to be me than you.

THE ORANGE GIRLS OF CORK

In every shop, but more especially
The chemists, in their uniform of shapely suit,
White blouse, high heels and maculate make-up:
Max Factor Medium, whatever the sun-index.
Achieving glamour always, even in those
Hustling weeks up to Christmas, cold outside,
Fragrant-warm within; the banjo-fiddle duo
Next to the Munster Arcade or Cash's,
Scarfed tight at this time of the year.
The expert boys selling the glottal '*Echo*':
Species resident here and nowhere but here.

Oh but they were the stars: the elder sisters
In the Pleiades of Woolworths-girls,
They'd stepped straight out of the pictures
At the Pavilion or Capitol or Ritz,
Still made up for the American night.
Most miraculous, they have survived
Through all the changes. They alone have held
Their station through our seasons of Filofax
And mobile phones and cappuccino,
Rolling their Cork *r*s and eyes at everyone.

PHILOMELA

If things got any worse, she'd take up knitting
and sit across the hearth from his thin-lipped silence,
murmuring a new language and logic:
Cast on purlwise. Knit one stitch through back
of loop. Yarn around needle. C6B, P6, K2.
And it would all mean nothing to him,
such woman's writing. No more than love had.

So what should the picture on her peplum be?
On the whole, a sorry scene: not exactly
a tongue cut out, but the steady rooting up
of a grove of voices, one after the other.
And as her fingers filled the details in,
his hawkish eyes will fill with tears, hearing
her absent humming from across the fire.

THE WIND IN THE WILLOWS

It couldn't have been written in our neck
of the woods, because – misnamers of everything –
we called them salleys and used them magically
to divine water or, not sparing their rods,
improve children. We had no moles, nosing up
from their sweet below-ground homes. The stoats, yes,
that invaded the big house, but we called them
weasels and abetted their vicious forays
down rabbit-holes. Good old squirely Mr Badger
with his pipe and slippers we suspected
of giving the cows TB and breaking
people's legs. The first badger I ever saw
was dead, thrown on a ditch near the monastery
of Timoleague, by the grey shining seashore:
a colour photograph in black-and-white.
On that same March day I also saw
a Mass-rock for the first time, and a
leprosarium, facing across the bay
towards Courtmacsherry, at the haunted house
where the poltergeist or poltergeists
cooked sausages at the mid-hour of night.

Westward along that road, near Clonakilty,
there still leans on its side the great boat-skeleton,
where waders beak-poke at the silver mud.
There is nothing, simply nothing, quite so worth doing
as messing about with waterside debris.

GROWING UP WITH CULLEN FEIS

The heel-to-toe batter of the hammering hornpipe
Mutes by a swift Cinderella-change to cross-garters
For the high-leg-reaching, silent reel, as if
The feet's speaker has suddenly gone dead.
Tension mounts: the bitter flusteredness
Of the dancing mothers – *Majella! Where's your cape?* –
Urging back more and more from the Coal-Quay call
Of the tinkers' stalls – 'apples and oranges
And ripe bananas!' – as the crimson-Celtic, ringleted,
Bone-kneed small girls grow through the evening
Into the distant, black-stocking hauteur
Of the long, long-legged senior teenagers.
The judge is incorruptible, undistractable,
His eyes fixed low on the yielding ash-boards,
Sprung like a good hurley. The heart-beat
Of the accompanists never falters either.
Unchanging too the backdrop to Singleton's field:
Caherbarnagh in Munster blue, Clara greener,
And the mocking conic profile of The Paps.

SHELLS OF GALICE

I like to set this modest test for scientists
who'll follow after, to wash some influence
into the future. I carry shells from one
seashore to another: from the Atlantic sweep
in front of the Riazor hotel, beneath
the excited lights of Deportiva,
to hide them in the silence of Dunquin

or on the cold, eastward-facing coast
of Lindisfarne. I've left Irish mussel-shells
exposed to the midday sun at Ostia.
Once I placed a pale-pink sea urchin
with all its fragile porcelain-like stipples
to take its chance high on a limestone mountain.
How are they going to account for it,

archaeologists in the years to come?
Will they guess that someone intervened
and tampered with geology's design,
the no-pace-perceived drift of continents?
Or will they see a different pattern in it,
how love and whim and irrational attachment
make us keep moving things from place to place.

THE SEA! THE SEA!

It must be that the rays reflected upwards
from the waves make the skin burn faster
than on sand. Afterwards, as you lie
half-listening to the soughing and the laughter
of unseen children, your slit eyes rest on
an Ambre Solaire-broiled arm, thrown there,
a few inches off and folded round your head:
a baked salmon, speckled, glistening
and succulent on top when the foil is opened,
but underneath veined and grey and sodden
where the molten oil's congealing on the towel.

RHUBARB, RHUBARB

We went up to Rockchapel, the two of us,
myself and Paddy Hickey; and because
he arranged a drive back with someone else,
I came home early, only stopping
at Curtin's shop to buy a bunch of rhubarb.

Still all right: still before the end of July
when rhubarb turns bitter and the days
get shorter, and well before you start
to count the dates from the darkening evenings
to the end of summer when they put back up

the big green wood shutters in Normandy
and children face for school again, and you throw out
July's *Irish Times*'s at the end of August.

VISITING THE BIRTHPLACE OF AODHAGÁN Ó RATHAILLE

for the Kellys and Heaneys

We got directions from a man in socks
asleep in front of 'Coronation Street'
who followed us to the door with a kind
of generous wistfulness, and then worked our way
up along the mountain road past Lisheen Cross
to reach the place itself, easily known
by its limestone monument. We set to,
taking photographs from different angles,
getting as much fuschia in as possible
and were just setting off (we had
a boat to catch) when the sound of a car
distracted us. It was audible long before
it rolled around the bend towards us
without benefit of silencer. I knew
the driver from somewhere and he knew me
as a friend. 'Come here,' he said with urgency,
'I have something to show you.' We climbed
through holly and early blackberries
into a small garden, in front of broken windows,
and followed him through the jagged glass
into a restored room: new orange plaster,
radiators and power-points. 'The lads
going home from school throw stones at it.
Because it's empty they think it's nobody's.
Once they lit a fire on the new boards below.
What kind of neighbours is it we have at all?'

I wasn't sure what to suggest, or any way
that we might help. He'd told the Guards
but they weren't interested. He'd sell it
if he could, but who would buy it now,
this half-wrecked bit of renovation?

It was coming on to rain, and time for us
to go, so he backed out of the way,
into the field-gap by the monument.
And as we drove back down towards Béal na Díge
I wondered who would want to fix a house
in that wet place of all earthly places.

THE SALLEY GARDENS

after Quasimodo

But how could we have sung our songs
with foreign heels upon our hearts,
amid the dead dumped in the squares
on the ice-stiffened grass: the lamb-cry
of children, the black scream
of the mother who came across her son
crucified on a telegraph pole?

On the branches of willows, like a jacket
hung by a worker on a hot day,
our harps too hung in sacrifice,
turning lightly in the grey wind.

THE COMPANY OF THE DEAD

It's natural that they would feel the cold
much more than we do; but that is partly
what makes them such good company.
They draw closer, rubbing their hands,
and praise the fire: 'That's a fine fire you've down.'

Also, they've no unrealised agendas,
their eager questions no barbed implications.
They're no trouble round the place, their only wish
now to get warmer: apart, that is, from wishing
that they'd kept warmer while they had the chance.

USEFULNESS

It was Jim McMahon who first pointed out
that you never come across a bald tinker,
nor do you ever see one in old age.
So the polite man in the hat who knocked
at the door and asked if he could have a look
at the contents of the shed, being fifty-odd,
was as old as they get. As we were going through
the junk, he picked up a bicycle pump,
remarked, 'This is no use, is it?' and,
when I agreed, he dropped it in his bag.
Next he picked up an old kitchen pan,
scrutinized it and said, 'This is no use, is it?'
and, when I said it wasn't, threw it away.

Now I wish I'd asked him while I had him
what things are for, or how he assessed their value,
since these are matters of much greater urgency
for the short-lived who have to make snap-judgements
and can't afford that often to be wrong.

G.

After her parents died when she was young
I nursed her to her present size,
Watching with silent pride
Her learning to smile and notice,
Admiring her limbs as they grew longer.
I let her grow, to see the turnout
Of her particular lineaments
Before I named her. Later on,
When she wanted to move out as teenagers do,
I found her a flat in the suburbs
Where occasionally I visited her
In the evenings without anyone knowing.
Now, finally, the happy day has come
When I see that she is ready to live up
To the name I gave her in honour of
A venerable family tradition
By calling her Grievance.

SIMON THE CYRENIAN

In the end, it's hard to know what to think
of him: doing the right thing because he was
press-ganged into it, but doing it none the less.
Or did he make things worse in the long term,
prolonging the agony with his inadequate help
and then returning to his own business?

Like me, the time I stood and talked
with the man from Lauragh, trying to explain
where he could get his birth certificate.
He was so slow on the uptake, I couldn't
spare the time and made my excuses.

As I hurried away, I took great care
not to turn back; but still I could feel them:
his eyes burning desperately as I retreated,
deep into the cross-beam of my shoulders.

ISLANDMAGEE CASTLE

for James Simmons

It is a castle, according to the map,
and you can find your way to it by climbing through
from the Crawfords' cattle-sheds. Right enough,
it has a Norman-looking arch over the gap
which must be where the window was, though now
it's just six feet of stone, barely hanging
together. The calves are nudging at
the hay-wisps round its base, oblivious to

What lies behind them: oyster-catchers
crying down at the shingle beach; sheer blue
between them and the green of Portmuck island,
and Ailsa Craig beyond. Once I stumbled
through there, trying to keep my feet, and found myself
face-to-face with a furtive-looking character,
his double-breasted coat hugged close around him.
'A gun,' I thought. He opened his coat

Revealing a colander of mushrooms.
'Take as many as you want for your Ulster fry,'
he said. 'Sure the fields are full of them this weather.'

SERAUNS

– Derevaun Seraun! Derevaun Seraun! (*from 'Eveline' by James Joyce*)

'The phrase is probably gibberish but phonetically like Irish.' (*Brendan O'Hehir*)

I couldn't see things, even when they were
right under my fingers; that's what was wrong.
Unlike Denis John who could make out
every hiding clump of shamrock, set tight
into gelid March grass-mud, or who could fill
a sweet-gallon with blackberries in half the time
it took me to cover the bottom enough
to stop them riddling around. He'd devote
himself to things, entirely set on picking
yellow primroses to give away, until
the big bunch stretched to translucent tightness
the webs between his thumbs and forefingers.

Do you remember those small grubs we looked for
to fish with? That is what serauns were.
He could find them too, pale below the wet earth,
freezing, hardly warm enough to twist
on his palm. Maybe out of this same failing
I have been lonely for fear of settling
for what was near to hand, which is why
I come upon myself repeatedly, sitting
in airport lounges, wishing I was back.

THE POTATO-GATHERERS

(on the painting by George Russell, AE)

They know what they're doing at the worst of times,
these three unpraying desperadoes
on home ground. No time to notice
the sun's orange angelus at their backs,
any more than we, halfway back to them,
used to pause for the grey shine in October skies
as the digger clattered past, anointing us
with wormly wet earth and withered-white
potato-plant pipes as we clutched for the seed,
for cold gold in the seam of gutter.
In that impressionist twilight, you can't make out
their fingers; even their bent backs you'd see better
with our millennial 20-20 sight
from a west-bound jet over Belmullet.

EVERYBODY LOVES PAT BOONE

The painful glamour of male childhood was
The elder sisters' friends. Who was the one
(She left Euthymol in the bathroom:
You put it in your mouth and spat it out,
Afraid you'd been poisoned, as perhaps
In the long term you had) with fair hair,
Friend of a friend, whose silver tongue
Made that confident and adult judgement:
'Everybody loves Pat Boone'?

TRACE ELEMENTS

It doesn't take much: grown careless
in old age, the outlaw Gisli
was tracked down by the parings
he whittled idly from his stick
as he walked along. A good disguise
is called for: something better than Tristan
calling himself Tantris; or than growing
a beard, bearing in mind what happened
when I shaved my beard off,
half-fancying the thought of
keeping it in a box, or sticking it
to a sheet of cardboard as maybe
a Christmas novelty. It might, I thought,
even survive me. But it wasn't
like that at all: although I cut it
with considered snips, it shattered,
amounting in the end to nothing more
than a small grey dusty pile,
hardly big enough to stay
visible on the towel round my neck.
So I brushed it fast into the bin,
before it reminded somebody of something worse.

BURNING FURZE

from the Irish of Liam Ó Muirthile

My Easter fire's a living furze-bush
burning by a ditch in Treesfield.
I don't know if it's native furze
or invader's gorse that yields before
my slasher's blade, from root
to golden head this time of year.
I breathe the honey fragrance,
then thrust it on the pile
and a smokecloud erupts
with a fist of hay and diesel.
I'm an incinerator, making room
for new growth; but when the flame
dies down, the charred limbs left
burnt black recall
the suddenness of death,
bodies swallowed by the blaze
on the road to Basra.

MEDIEVAL LOVE-DIPTYCH

for John Mole at 60

1. THE ANGLO-SAXON FISH RIDDLE

My beloved is my dwelling-place,
he is so talkative.
My house, the river, 's never silent,
taciturn tenant though I am.
Fate arranged that we travel together.

I swim faster than him, more strongly;
but he has more stamina. Sometimes
I have to pause for breath; but he
keeps running. I am within him, always,
while I live. Our parting will be death for me.

2. THE MIDDLE ENGLISH SEDUCER

No more will you, sweet lady,
twinkle with those eyes.
I did the like all through my youth,
once and twice and thrice.
Long loved, long implored,
bought expensively –

Door, stop creaking!
Keep quiet! Be still!
Gate, inside your boundary
I've had all my will.

GOOD FENCES MAKE

The history of our quickset hedge is this:
When Pat Joe Morley asked Denis Dansel
If he could take some slips of the vivid laurel
That grew along his ditchtop, Con Lehane
Planted them carefully, to perfection,
One foot apart the whole length of our road.

Four years later, those flat-lying cuttings
Have stood up and spread and joined together
In a thick phalanx that screens the whole garden.
Now Con is gone, his short bout of cancer ended,
And Dansel, after three years' forgetfulness,
Lies in unmarked ground by the wall of the Old Graveyard.

CELEBRITIES

'Tuohy, a small moustached man whose life was to end in suicide, amused Joyce at first and later bored him by urging him to write a best-seller.' (Ellmann, *James Joyce*)

I broke off a branch of hard spines
Of blackthorn so her binoculars
Could play over the distant glint
Of river. 'They've found the body.'

I could just make out small laborious
Figures in the field behind the house
He'd stormed out of two nights before,
Accused of cheating at cards.

– *Go after him, Jim.* – He'll never do it.
– *It's his claim to fame.* Twenty years later,
It's two students laughing over martinis.
– *We're bad for eachother. But we find*

Everyone else so tedious and opportunist.
Depression got her first; but he'd caught it
Like a heavy cold, and it killed him too.
My copy of the *Duino Elegies* has a name

At the front of somebody who bored me
Beyond all bearing. His hopeless attempts
At 'Stranger on the Shore' on clarinet
Were always to the accompaniment

Of his own doubled-up laughing. I worked out
A route home where I wouldn't meet him
And watched his back in triumph. The last time
I saw him I did dutifully speak, but he didn't.

His eyes were full of tears. *We were sad*
In that sweet air that basks in sunlight.
But who among the angelic orders heard us
When we cried? No one. No one listens.

THE DRUID'S FOSTERSONS' DEBATE AT TEAMHAIR

Said Deroil, 'Can you see what I see? Swords
stained with blood of war, and massed men marching.'
'It is no such thing,' said Darail, 'but the memory
of the huge oaks we passed by yesterday.
The blood is in your head.' 'Then what about
the traffic of royal chariots they travel in?'
'You're imagining again. They are not chariots
but the windblown ringforts you see everywhere
in these parts.' 'If that is what they are,
why then are they full of brilliant white shields?'
'Not shields. Those are the limestone crags
that were the doorposts.' 'If it's all so simple,
why are there red-armed spears thrust out above
the black breastplates of that thronging army?'
'Those are the stags and wild bulls of Duhallow
with their meshed horns and antlers cast aloft.'

OLD BLUE-EYES

You look as if you've been crying,
but you haven't particularly.
It's only ageing:

that great leveller of greens,
blues, browns and even those
fetching, not quite matching, sets.

The only benefit is you can cry away
and no one will know the difference,
which at this stage is something we all could use.

CHOUGH

Old redfoot-jackdaw, you know where
to pick your retirement home, drawn
by the artist's tax concessions
to the southern sweep of the Great Blasket
where Europe's tourists, safe in their fleeces
or Aran ganseys, cower against
the August squall. When the rain stops
they'll hear you, cryking behind them
somewhere off the moss-soft beaten track:
or, when the sun's come out again,
outside the clubhouse in Ballybunion
where you while away the summer afternoon
in the company of other shy exiles.
What taxman could make you out down there?

THE TWISTING OF THE ROPE

A man lived down by the castle
called Tim John Batt. His father was Batt Murphy
who delivered the post on foot and went by boat
every weekend to run in Wales and London,
so their long low farmhouse was filled with trophies.
His mother's people were poets from Kiskeam.

In the time when hay was drawn in by float,
Tim John was attended by a team of children.
To keep them safe, he'd punch an indentation
at the front of the big haycock and strap them down
with the hayrope he threw diagonally from the back,
pulled tight to stop the cleanings falling off.

Nearly fifty years on, I walk those fields again,
now to read the summer sky. At midnight
it's all under control: Vega blue in the heights;
the Plough's steady eyes upon its furrow.
But when I wake up in the early hours,
it's all gone haywire: the Triangle

has toppled westward; Orion's on his face,
his Dog above him, sniffing anxiously
for signs of life before it dawns. Later again,
the whole thing has gone, the Dog fading last,
his bark growing less audible until
in the end you can hardly even hear

the music of the spheres. Yes, many things
have changed since then, it's true. The corncrake's gone;
the cuckoo's on her way. Tim John, who'd forced
the jawing horse back towards the haybarn,
is now himself backing out of the picture,
twisting the long hayrope as he goes.

LOVE'S MEDIUM

The Anglo-Saxon elegist observes
that it isn't difficult to separate
what wasn't joined properly to start with.

It's unlike that with you, able as you are
to sit apart across the room and still
be together. But as your glances meet,

the waves they pass through invisible
as radio, they do not interfere
with the reception of the rest of us,

caught in graceful crossfire. How? And how
can you call 'Wulf, my Wulf!' with unmoving lips?
I see a figure somewhere in the distance

who raises an axe, then lets it fall through
it's own weight so it's half-way up again
before I hear the heart-thud and shudder

and realise: he's not felling trees;
he is making wood. Who said 'Love unspoken
is more binding'? Who said it first? And who will say it last?

The Wedding of Elanor Dymott and Simon Marshall
11 August 2001

FOR ELLEN (20) IN COUNTY CORK

You, I imagine, this new autumn morning
are somewhere by the sea; but here, inland,
it's another of those stifling days
when, though the wind is strong enough to bend
the fuchsia over, we can hardly breathe.

Our ageing Worcester apple-tree which, less
than twenty years ago, had so much fruit
we'd give a cumbersome boxful to the neighbours,
now bears fewer than half a dozen in all.
But still each year I make a point of eating
one at least, to keep alive the flavour
of those early days of productivity.

As time goes by (I've remarked on this before)
I'm becoming something of a specialist
at lamenting anniversaries, year in, year out;
but here is one – this morning, this fervent breeze –
which wakes with nothing but enthusiasm.

Oxford, 11 September 1998

GOALKEEPERS

Custodians. The last line of defence,
Most celebrated lineage of heroes.
Tony 'The Dummy' Reddan of Tipperary,
Whose farm-cap kept the sun out of his eyes
So the ball thumped safely into his heart
Of blue and gold where his generous hand
Could close on it. Art Foley of Wexford
Who made the great save from Ring in '56.
Kilkenny's all-time All-stars, Walsh and Skehan.

When I first read the papers, Cork's goalie
Was a legend whose brother I got to know
In Oxford a generation later.
He lived towards the bottom of Divinity,
In a houseful of quiet, single, courteous,
Drinking Irishmen. He never boasted of
His celebrated brother: even discouraged
Talk of him. And one cold January night
He jumped from Folly Bridge into the Thames.

FINNÉIGEAS

Though failing in his lifelong quest for wisdom
when the boy burned his finger on the salmon
and licked the pain, he got the better bargain
in the end. For, in his declining years,
it was his fireside that friends gathered by
to listen to the learning of his failures,
while know-all Finn, after whom were named
mountain ranges and battlefields, was hated
by all for the miseries he caused and suffered,
and there was praise only for the man who'd kill him.
And ultimately Finn's wisdom told him this:
no one loves a wise man, not even himself.

FRA ALBERIGO'S BAD FRUIT

(Dante, *Inferno* xxxiii, 91–157)

On we went, till we reached a place where frost
remorselessly confined another group, whose heads
didn't look down but were stuck twisted backwards.

It was crying itself that hindered their ability
to cry, and the misery, impacted at their eyes 95
of ice, ingrown, intensified the agony:

Because the first tears would freeze into a knot,
and, like hard-glass, opaque contact lenses,
filled up the whole space under the eyelids.

And, though the frost had taken every ounce 100
of feeling from my face, making it
like solid muscle to the fingers,

I thought now I felt some touch of breeze,
and asked: 'Master, where can this have come from?
Surely no wind is active in these depths?' 105

Virgil answered, 'Soon we'll reach a place
where you'll see with your own eyes the source
from which this strange current reaches us.'

Then one of those suffering from the frozen eye-crust
called out to us: 'You two souls, so evil 110
that you're on your way to the utmost depths of Hell,

Peel off, I beg of you, the hard veils from my face,
so I can release to some extent the grief
trapped in my heart, before the tears freeze over again.'

I said to him, 'If you want me to do this, 115
tell me who you are; and, if I do not then anoint your eyes,
may I indeed have to go to the iciest part of Hell.'

'All right,' he said. 'I'm Alberigo, the Jovial Friar,
who called for "Fruit!" as the agreed signal to kill.
Now I'm fed here with an even sourer fruit.' 120

'But,' I asked him, 'are you then dead already?'
He answered, 'I can't speak for what is happening to
my physical body in the world above;

'But it's a privilege of this Ptolemaic Hell
that often souls fall down into its depths 125
before Death has severed them from life.

'And, to persuade you more readily to remove
the jagged glass tears off of my face,
let me tell you that, at the very instant

'when the soul turns traitor, its body is possessed 130
by a demon that stays in charge of it
until its allotted time of life is over;

'But the soul falls straight down to this abyss.
Take this shade who winters here behind me –
maybe his body is still on earth as well. 135

'If you've just come, you'll know. Is Branca d'Oria
still up there? For it's many a long year
since he was shut here in this fellowship.'

'You must be lying to me,' I said to him.
'Branca d'Oria's still alive; he eats and drinks 140
and sleeps and puts his clothes on him.'

'It's not true. Michael Zanche had not yet arrived
in that upper ditch, the Malebranche,
where the vortex of the clinging pitch is boiling,

'When this Branca left a devil in his body 145
in the world above; the same with one of his cousins
who collaborated in his treachery.

'But come on; reach out your hand to me;
open my eyes.' But I didn't open them for him;
and being boorish towards the likes of him was courtesy. 150

People of Genoa! Strangers to every decency
and disfigured by every vice conceivable,
why are you not wiped clean off the face of the earth!

For down with the very worst soul from Romagna
I came on one of yours who, because of his deeds, 155
already bathes in Cocytus in spirit
while up in the world he seems bodily alive.

SEDGE-WARBLERS AT BECKLEY, JUNE 2002

for John and Jean Flemming

This terrible summer, we must make the most
of every sunlit evening. So we walked
by the new fibre track above the reeds,
mocked by their extraordinary goatsong,
so unlike the song of birds. And such odd
accompanists: free of all shyness,
they'd start to call when we came within earshot,
untroubled by our talk or peering for them,
and stop, disappointed, as we left.
Sometimes we would watch the reeds swaying,
sure sign of their presence, a sign of life,
but never the birds themselves: strange acrobats
that made their long poles waver at the top
by swinging at their base. Or so it seemed.

Two larks filled with their back-dreaming song
the central space marked out by church steeples:
Islip and Oddington and Fencott.
Even shaded eyes could not pick them out,
well as the sound located them. But if
you half-closed your eyes, as once you did
to spread the light of candles in the church
from oval glow to stretched-out yellow pool,
you had a better chance of seeing them:
just to one side of where the unbroken rapture
seemed to come from, a few degrees away,
a dancing point, a concentration of
the cloud. No more than that, yet everything
your eyes' attentiveness had reached out for.

ANY LAST REQUESTS

i.m. Pádraig Ó hIcí

But I was here on Broadway,
  Carrying bricks for load,
When they carried out her coffin
  Down the Old Bog Road.
(*Theresa Brayton*)

This sunny October morning, I notice
for the first time that the swallows are gone,
well gone, though I never saw them going.
I'm busy brushing wood preservative
into my English garden fence, while you
are being driven for the final time,
down from Eagloune, past the ditch where
on party nights it was so dark
the shushing visitors couldn't find their cars.
I should be driving with you
past your untended loganberry beds,
to negotiate the dangerous northward turn
by the forge. It no longer matters
that the wind gets through the broken panes
which you had better things to do
than to get fixed. I think
it no longer matters; but then I'm not there.

No other house where I was
so unconditionally welcome,
even after failing you in one of your
far-fetched lifelong enterprises:
your strange soprano 'hello' always
a misleading prelude to the letters
you rooted for under the *Saol*s and cushions
and books and *Examiner*s. And every time
I failed to visit, no less welcome

the next time. But what happens now?
When I next push my way past the dog
and turn the key that is always in the lock,
I will at last be greeted by silence.
'Bhfuil tú sa bhaile a Phádraig?
Are you home?'

VANISHING-POINTS

for Robert and Badral Young

Safe in an armchair in the dentist's surgery,
you observe your daughter's treatment:
being cruel to be kind again. You fix on
the criss-cross of her trainers' soles
in the foreground, on past her brave socks,
grazed knees, school jumper and clasped hands
to the vanishing-point that is her head,
laid back. It is the same perspective as
in the photograph of the thrown-away body
of the young Taliban soldier. His trainers,
similarly foregrounded, look as if
they could be the same designer label.
But this vanishing-point is past his head, way out
in the impassive desert sands towards Kabul.

25.11.2001

THE MULE DUIGNAN

Nowadays it always rains in Bristol,
and every night, trying to get to sleep,
I hear it, looking beyond to the lights
winking over the Clifton Bridge, like the lights
of the shoreline seen from the Irish mailboat.

It helps me to drop off if I go over
details from childhood, like the big key
of acrid cast iron that shut and opened
the front door. I find it strange to still remember
that it opened clockwise, and locked the way
you'd expect to open it. Most often
I think back to a December night
when my small sister crept into bed with me,
shivering. We listened to our father's voice,
emphatic and quiet: 'If the cow does die tonight,
we'll have to sell up and go.' We prayed ourselves
to sleep. In the morning the wind woke us
and we all went out together to the stall.
The cow was standing up, eating hay.
And then for the first and only time I saw
my parents embracing. I hate that country:
its poverties and embarrassments
too humbling to retell. I'll never ever
go back to offer it forgiveness.

When my father died at last, the place
was empty. I went back to bury him,
then turned the key in the lock and dropped it
in the estate-agent's letterbox
and turned my back for ever on it all.